I Hate
Studying

I Hate Studying

Calvinn Tay

PARTRIDGE
A Penguin Random House Company

To order additional copies of this book, contact
Toll Free 800 101 2657 (Singapore)
Toll Free 1 800 81 7340 (Malaysia)
orders.singapore@partridgepublishing.com

www.partridgepublishing.com/singapore

CONTENTS

Preface: School Doesn't Teach You Everything............................ 13

    Why Go to School? 14

    Here is Why 14

    So What's The Problem?................................. 15

    My Concern 16

    Things are Changing Fast 17

    Some Succeed.. 17

    Do You Want to Get Left Behind? 18

    The Bridge Builder 18

Introduction: I Hate Studying................................ 21

    A Comment from Einstein 23

    Learn, Unlearn, Relearn 23

    For My Friends 24

    This Book 25

    The Price... 27

Chapter 1: Believe and You Will Achieve 29

    A Heart Break Lesson................................. 30

    Fresh New Eyes 32

    Half Full or Half Empty? 33

    Help Won't Come. You've to Find It................ 34

1 Mark 35

Small Things Make A Difference 37

Chapter 2: Give Me One Reason 39

Your Brain 101 40

A Journey Inwards 41

What do you want to do? 42

Why do you want to do it? 43

How can you do it? 43

Have You Found Your Reason? 44

The Wolf and The Rabbit 45

Do What You Want 46

Passion 47

I Must Do It 48

The Man Who Had Nothing 49

Chapter 3: Control Yourself 51

Emotions Are Guides 52

Anger is A Terrible Master 52

Anger is A Powerful Servant 53

Nothing to Fear, but Fear Itself 55

Pain of The Past 56

Feeling Good Isn't Being Happy 57

Make Your Body Feel Good 59

Keep Smiling 61

Listen to yourself 61

Chapter 4: Dare to Dream 64

Fortune Favors the Bold 65

As Simple As Possible 66

Leverage 67

80-20 Rule 68

The Difference That Makes The Difference............. 69

You've to Walk Before You Run............................... 70

The View is Nicer on Top.. 71

Putting It All Together 72

Chapter 5: Learn.. 74

Studying is Not Learning 75

Knowledge is Not Power 76

Learn and Grow 77

How Do You See The World?................................... 77

You Look but You Don't See.................................... 78

You Hear But You Don't Listen 81

Talk is Cheap 83

Practice Makes Perfect... 85

Relearn and Unlearn 85

Here is What I Did 86

Be Willing to Make Mistakes.................................. 87

Afterword... 89

A Return to Love... 89

Which Genius Are You? 90

Imperfection is Our Perfection 93

My Last Gift 95

About the Author... 97

To those who I have met in life and those who I'll meet in life.
Thank you all for this book.

For those who are willing to learn, unlearn and relearn…

PREFACE:

School Doesn't Teach You Everything

The sound of my alarm woke me up as usual. I have got to remind myself to switch it off tonight.

I'll switch off the alarm not to get ready for the day, but to sleep again. I don't know why I'm such a light sleeper. My friends could sleep pass an earthquake. I wish I could sleep like that.

"Wake up! Or you'll be late for school!" A different alarm rang. My mom would wake me up when the alarm failed. It was like this every day. I'm getting kind of tired of it. I see no need for the alarm anyways. She was the one that would wake me up.

I would get ready for 7 hours of school. The thought of it always made me lose my appetite. That's why I always skipped breakfast. I would have it later during recess.

"Why do you always need me to wake you up?" she asked curiously.

"I just don't like to go to school." I replied. I wore my socks and tied my tie while looking at the uniform that I have been wearing for 5 years.

"Even though you don't like it, you still have to go. Do well in your exams and you'll get a good job. Then you will have a good life," she persuaded.

"School only teaches us to take exams. I don't see how my exam results will help me get more money in the future or a better life."

"Just get good results in your exam and you'll see."

I tied my shoe laces and got my bag, another day of pointless studying so that I can do well the exams. I got on my bicycle and rode to school. The only thing worth waiting for in that place was my friends.

Why Go to School?

So here is a student's point of view. I have to wake up at 6am for five days a week. I have to sit in a classroom for 7 hours and stay back for extra classes to learn things that I'm probably never going to use in my life.

And I have to memorize all of that stuff into my brain, so that I may know how to answer during the exams. To me, going to school isn't about learning. It is about memorizing. To me, it is a waste of time and also boring.

Here is Why

You see, the whole purpose of the school is to prepare students for jobs. That's the main reason the school was built for. It is to provide education to the public so that there can be more specialists for the country.

If there were no schools, many can't read or speak. They also might not know basic math to do business. So these skills must be imported from other countries.

School plays an important role in the development of the country. Without it, there will be no development. But I'm not saying that the school system is perfect. Honestly speaking it isn't. Nothing created by man will ever be perfect.

The school allows locals to take over the economy, politics and also social aspects of the country. It might have been full proof during the industrial age, the age which the system was introduced, but not today.

The school acts as a filter for companies to find employees as well. Let's say 10,000 student attends a university. 10% of them will get a GPA of 3.50 and above. So companies will have 1000 candidates to choose from.

Going to school might not get you the job you want. In fact, it might not get you a job at all. But nonetheless, it is much more better to be with a degree than without one. School helps you to be employed.

So What's The Problem?

The problem is very simple. The school system has influence many to hate the system and also to hate studying. That's because the school is too focused on help the students find a job and have forgotten that we are now in a different age.

They think that results are more important than the actual learning process. So memorizing is the method commonly used by the school to help students get good results for the exam. Students either hate studying or don't study at all.

Learning just isn't fun anymore. That's why students today hate going to school. After university or college, many students can't wait to get out of school thinking that they will have a nice job and a good life.

So you have a degree in Accounting, what do you think your first salary will be? RM 4000 per month? Maybe RM3000? It will be somewhere between RM2000 and RM 2500. Can you afford the car you want? Can you buy the big house you dreamed of?

Besides that, you have to compete for your job as well. What should a company choose you when there are so many other smart graduates? What makes you so special? What makes you so unique and different from the rest?

That's just one part of the problem. The school system teaches things that are right and that are wrong, so students always believe that there is only one right answer and one wrong answer.

This takes away the creativity of students to come up with solutions to hard problems that they will face later in life. Life is not the same as school. There is always more than one right answer, but students believe that there is only one. How are they suppose to compete in this world of technology if they only know one right answer?

My Concern

I'm not pointing fingers saying that this is anyone's fault. I'm just saying this is what I happened to noticed in my 12 years of school. I'm just worried about what might happen to future students if the problem continues.

If they hate studying, they will hate learning. If they keep on believing that there is only one right answer to every problem, then they will fail to see the opportunities that the world today has to offer.

They will fail to find their own uniqueness. Most of all, they will live their entire life believing that they are just average. They will lose the qualities and characteristics that will differentiate them from the crowd. Their light to shine dies before they even know that they have it.

"Death is not the greatest loss in life. The greatest
loss is what dies inside us while we live."

-Norman Cousins

Things are Changing Fast

Since the internet, information is moving at a faster rate. And it will only get faster. The world today is borderless. So information travels from one place to another in a very quickly.

A lot of things can now happen in one day. You can try buying different newspapers that have the same date just to see how many things had happened in the last 24 hours.

If you don't want to waste your money on this, then you can just stop Facebook for 24 hours. After 24 hours, check back to see how much posts and statues that you have missed.

I bet you can imagine the amount of information from these two examples. Quite a lot isn't it? How are the student today going to adapt to these changes when all they ever know is to memorize and choose the right answer?

"It is not the strongest of the species that survives,
nor the most intelligent that survives. It is
the one most adaptable to change."

-Charles Darwin

Some Succeed

Yes, it is true that many have indeed benefitted from the school system. Many lawyers, doctors, engineers, and scientists have started as students in school. They have a secure high paying job and are able to live quite a comfortable life.

There is no denying this fact, but what about those that don't do well in school. What about those that can't get good enough results in school to become lawyers, engineers, scientists, or doctors?

Not to mention in the world today, the economy isn't that good now is it? What about the increasing unemployment rate? What about those that can't get good results in their exam? Are they destined to work menial jobs for the rest of their life?

I really want the answer to be "No". But only they themselves can choose their own future. But the good thing is that it is possible for someone without good results to make it big in life.

This has been proven by many famous icons. Andrew Carnegie, Steve Jobs, Bill Gates, Henry Ford have done just that.

So, it seems it is possible to get rich even though you don't have good results in school. Now I want you to know that it is possible to get good results without studying.

Do You Want to Get Left Behind?

The world is moving forward in an ever changing pace. We can't predict the future, but we can prepare for it. I will be blunt with you. If you can't learn to adapt to the ever changing world, you will only be left behind.

The choice is still yours. You can choose to do what others are doing. Or you can make your own future. You can choose who you want to be. But you have got to learn.

The Bridge Builder

I don't have to write this book. But I want to. There is a poem I loved to share with you. It is one of the poems that had led me to write this book for you.

The poem is called "The Bridge Builder", written by Will Allen Dromgoole. Read it a few times. I believe that it will convince you that I just want the best for you.

> *This chasm, that has been naught to me,*
> *To that fair-haired youth may a pitfall be.*
> *He, too, must cross in the twilight dim;*
> *Good friend, I am building this bridge for him."*

So my journey has ended. Now it is your turn. Let me show you how unique you are.

INTRODUCTION:

I Hate Studying

"The time is up. Put down your pens, please. Make sure you wrote your name on the paper and stay where you are. I'll collect the papers now."

I'm awake, but I refuse to open my eyes. The paper is on the right side of my table while my head is on the left. I would have slept easier if I could still bring my pillow, too bad that the teacher didn't allow it anymore.

The teacher leaves the classroom. The students stand up and the whole room is filled with discussions. I could hear every conversation. It was the same in every school I've been to.

"Which question did you choose?"

"What did you write about?"

"What's the answer for No.37?"

I could hardly care less. I knew it didn't do well because I didn't study. There was nothing to fuss about. I accepted my fate.

"If you studied, then you would do well. If you didn't, you won't do well," advised my mom. She would always say this when I get bad results. I guess I will be hearing it again today.

There was a difference between my friends in SMK Alor Akarand my friends in SMK Teluk Chempedak. I see so many smart students worrying about their results. Even though they were A students, they felt like they weren't smart at all.

On the other hand, those in SMK Teluk Chempedak weren't as good as the ones in SMK Alor Akar. My friends in my old school wouldn't worry much about the results. They knew that they wouldn't do well, so there was no point in worrying about it.

The saddest thing that I saw was how both parties still doubted themselves. One of my friends in SMK Teluk Chempedak, Kin Tung was an amazing people's person. But he just didn't know it. The school didn't recognize his talent. He learned extremely fast and also had tons of friends everywhere. His connections were wide.

Another friend of mine was Ryan. He was the most disciplined guy that I had ever met. I had never seen him lose himself. He is always so happy and cheerful. I admired his humour and innocents.

In SMK Alor Akar, there were a lot of great squash players, very athletic and great guys. But they aren't very outstanding in their studies. Aiman is one of them. He is a strong, independent and matured teenager. Although he doesn't do very well, he is happy with his results.

There were misunderstood people as well. Students today are faced with more problems than ever before. The society that we live in are full of these problems, so they will affect the teens in the society too.

Jeevan was another friend I met that came from a rough background. But despite all that he went through, he is doing alright. He could turn out to be worse. He is a normal student, nothing outstanding about his results. To me, that itself is an extremely remarkable achievement. He had endured and experienced more pain than the average student. But still he turned out to be alright.

The characters and qualities of all the students are not recognized by the school. The school only care about exam results, but they failed to see what other things that students have to offer.

We don't learn in school anymore. We study. We are taught to follow orders and a fixed way to do things. This is just the way it is, so that employees are produced.

You see, not everyone is the same. Just as there are a lot of animals, there are different types of people that have different qualities. Studying is just a one way ticket to good results. It doesn't teach students to use their gifts.

That is why I hate studying.

A Comment from Einstein

"*Everyone is a genius. But if you judge a fish by its ability to climb a tree, it will live its whole life believing that it is stupid.*"
-Albert Einstein

He was talking about our education system. Every one of us is gifted with a talent that the school doesn't know about. Whether it is a good character, a kind heart, optimism or a good friend, the school doesn't test these things in the exam.

I believe that everyone is a genius. Everyone can get good results in school using their own genius. But they need to learn. And I will show you how. A fish might not be able to climb a tree, but we are humans.

Our limits are our own imagination.

Learn, Unlearn, Relearn

As I have said, the world is constantly changing. To survive in it, we have to learn how to adapt. We have to try new ideas that we never tried, do new things that we never did before. Change is not required, it is necessary. We need to change, or we'll be left behind.

It is not good enough that we learn. We must also unlearn, and relearn. There are too many things for us to know about. No matter how many books you've read, there will be something that you don't know.

Even though you may think you know something, you can always learn about something new. Relearning means having the humility to admit to your mistakes and change. We need to unlearn so that we let go of dying ideas and accept new ones.

Change is upon us. The school can't help you get a good life anymore. You have to do it yourself. The school can only help you get a job. It isn't perfect, nothing created by man ever was.

Just imagine how many people have graduated from college now. How many are qualified for the work that you are going to do? If you want to stay ahead, you have to learn something new and different, but that's just my point of view.

"The illiterate of the future are not those who can't read or write, but those who cannot learn, unlearn, and relearn."

-Alvin Toffler

For My Friends

As I have said, I had two groups of friends. The ones that are good in their studies and the one those aren't. Those in SMK Alor Akar do better in school than those in SMK Teluk Chempedak.

Those that aren't good in their studies will always go for what they want. But they might not have the skills possible yet. They know what they want to be. I was lucky to meet them, because I wouldn't be who I am today without them.

Those that are good in their studies will less likely do what they want. They are the good, obedient type that always does what they need to do. They will face an enormous amount of pressure and expectation of they continue to do so. When you have to do something you don't like, will you be happy doing it?

Both groups of student face the same problems in their school life and are more likely to face the same problems when they get out into the society.

Some don't have the courage to do what they want because they are scared of failure. Our school made students afraid to fail because you are punished if you made mistakes, while you're rewarded if you make none.

You will make mistakes in life. That's because you're human. When students are afraid to make mistakes, they are afraid to learn. They will never do things that they won't usually do. They will always cling to security and also stay in their comfort zone. There will be no progress.

The other problem with them is that they don't know how to use the things that they thought you in school, and use it to solve the problems in their life. School doesn't teach you this do they? They only teach you how to take an exam.

School fixes the questions to a few answers and only accepts the right ones, which is usually the only one. Students believe that there is and always will be only one right answer to every question. They failed to see the opportunities that are available to them.

I want a change. And it starts with this book.

This Book

I want my friends to know that there is more to them than just results. Your exam results don't determine your life. They only determine your job. You are a genius. You just don't know it yet.

I have given much effort in writing this book by myself. So I hoped that it will achieve one simple thing. If there is one thing that you have learnt from this book, please know that you are a genius. There is nothing in the world that you can't do. You are needed and you can make a difference.

This book will teach you how to get good results without studying. But we will take baby steps first. The last chapter in the book will show you how you learn, and how you can get the results you want in school without studying.

The other chapters are lessons that I have learnt from books and my experiences that will help you later in life. They are the core principles of any success story. So I share my knowledge with you.

This book isn't about how well I did in school. It is about my mistakes and how it can help you do better. If you are afraid to learn from your own mistakes, then learn from mine. I have made plenty along in these 11 years of school.

I will be challenging old ideas along the way. I hope that you will be kind enough to see from my point of view. Some books are meant to be read, others to be digested. In this book, there are advices that I gave myself over and over again. They have helped me make remarkable progress in school and also helped me finish this book.

I believe that you can do much more than what I have achieved. Just be you and always learn from mistakes, either yours or others.

"Wise is the one who learns from another's mistakes. Less wise is the one who learns only from his own mistakes. The fool keeps making the same mistakes again and again and never learns from them."
-Sri Sri Ravi Shankar

The Price

Nothing in the world is free. There is a price for everything that you do. If you want to use this method, please know that there is something you must do to make it possible.

You must be able to know your mistakes. You must accept them. And you must learn from them. Can you do that?

Learning can't be done without mistakes. That is how I have made the changes to my life. I had made mistakes. Now, it is your turn.

If you're willing to admit your mistakes and learn from them, then you will definitely succeed if you don't give up.

Learning isn't the same as studying. You don't need to memorise much because it will all come more naturally. You'll feel curious, excited and also restless in learning new things.

So, are you willing to pay the price to get good results without studying?

CHAPTER 1:

Believe and You Will Achieve

When I collected my Moral exam paper, my teacher said, "I know you don't like to study. But you are already in the game. So you can follow the rules and play, or you can quit playing."

I told myself, "I will win at the games, but I'll be using my own rules." I didn't say it out loud because I respected her. But I was thinking about it in my head.

I thought, "Why can't I get higher marks for my Moral? I've already gotten 38 this time and I didn't even study."

Needless to say, I was an extreme optimist. This was the major reasons that I wanted to do well in the upcoming SPM. I wanted to prove that I can get good results, but not with studying hard like everyone else.

So the challenge was accepted. I wanted my good results. But I didn't want to do all the homework that teachers gave. I didn't want to study late every night. I wanted to be able to have time for myself and friends. I wanted to do it on my own terms.

The first step in achieving anything is to believe you can. If you think you can, you'll do it. If you don't, you won't.

If a soldier does not believe that he can win the war. I don't think he would still fight in the war, right? But if there was even a small chance that he will be able to win the war, I'm sure that he will fight for it.

You won't do something if you believe you can't do it. This is true for everyone. So let me ask you. Would you get good results if you knew that you could not get it? No? That's the problem right here.

In this chapter, I will convince that you can get good results. Hope is what you need to believe and I will give you hope. I'll try my best to make you believe. Please try your best to believe.

> *"If you didn't achieve something, it is simply because you didn't believe enough."*
>
> *-Mario Novak*

A Heart Break Lesson

So the year was 2011, it was my PMR year. As all teenagers, I had a crush on a girl that was simply amazing to me at that time. I thought she was perfect. She was always very cheerful and very fun to be with.

Love blinded me. I thought that maybe, she was the one that could make me into a better person. I wasn't actually a nice guy back then. You could say that I was damaged, full of problems that weren't solved. I just didn't know that she was just the same as me.

So I was still in SMK Teluk Chempedak at that time. I had a crazy idea. I said to myself, "Why not transfer to her school next year?"

It was a crazy idea. But then again, maybe I wasn't thinking enough. I just went with it. To transfer to SMK Alor Akar with my PMR results, I need 4A's and above for my PMR. I aimed for 7A's because I want insurance. I wanted to make sure that I could get in the school.

At the beginning of the year, I didn't have such good results. But I did try to get good results without studying. It was this year that I knew about the fun of learning. I also knew about how powerful it can be.

When I got my PMR results in December, I was happy beyond compare. I got 7A's. I immediately applied for a transfer next year. I was able to transfer without much fuss. And I was enrolled into SMK Alor Akar in March.

So there I was, at the school where my crush was in. The first few months were considered one of those happy moments of the year. I even skipped classes to find her at her class. We were definitely the best of friends.

When I found out that she didn't felt the way I felt, I just lost it I guessed. I blamed myself every night for a week. I kept on telling myself how stupid I was to actually think that it would work. I guess she wasn't the one.

She liked one of my friends, and that was that. I understand why she did that. And I'm sorry for causing her such a need to do so. So for the first week after I found out, I did kind of regret my decision to transfer school. I had problem sleeping for the week. I just took me a while longer to get myself together.

Finally I had enough of the heart break and I told myself, "Are you going to let one girl ruin your life?"

Even though I did feel something for the girl, I couldn't deny that I had my whole life ahead of me. So, it was kind of pointless to let this small thing from making me feel sad for so long. I decide it was time to move on, but I didn't know how to do it, at that time.

I started thinking on the good things that had happened when I transferred into the school. It was a new environment for me. I also met new friends that helped me got by the tough time I had.

Jody, Li Ying, Tung Wei, Yan Shan, Jen Yi, and Phan Huey were amazing friends. They were as beautiful as they were smart. I'm glad to have met them. And I'm proud to call them my friends.

They boosted my confidence a lot. Before I met them, I felt uncomfortable being around girls. But ever since I spent so much time with these beautiful young ladies, I had a thought. Sure I didn't get the girl of my dreams, but I had gained 6 wonderful friends, which were girls. It was something I never thought I could have done.

The lesson in all of this is that if you want to change your life, you have to change the way you think. If I had just focused on the heart break that I had face, then I wouldn't be able to see the blessings I had.

Fresh New Eyes

If you to achieve something first, you must first believe that you can do it. To change your beliefs, you need to change the way you look at things. That's why I started with the story. I thought that it might help you remember these lessons.

Nobody can make you believe in anything but yourself. You believe in something because you had experienced it before, or you had seen it happened before.

I'm here to tell you that you can choose what to believe. You can also convince yourself to do so. I bet you think that you have no control over the things that you believe in. Well I'm here to tell you that you do.

Let's start lesson No. 1.

> *"Change the way you look at things and the things you look at will change"*
> -Wayne W. Dyer

Half Full or Half Empty?

So if I fill a glass half full with water and handed it to you, would you say it is half full or half empty? I'm not talking about positive thinking. There is no way you can be positive every time. You will think about negative things from time to time. This is what makes us human.

I'm talking about selective thinking. You have the ability to choose your own thoughts, therefore creating your own words, actions, habits, and eventually destiny. Now it all starts with thoughts because you won't do something if you don't believe you can.

If you learn how to change your perspective, or selectively think, you can change your destiny. It is that simple, but not that easy. It takes time and practice. So here are a few ways to get started.

Wake up in the morning and think about as many good things that might happen on that day. Remember I said might, not will. Let your imagination go crazy. It is a good way to get the day started, much better than your cup of morning coffee.

Life is the same as a glass that is half filled of water. It will always be that way. The question now is, "Which side of life do you want to see?"

Thinking about negative thoughts will bring you worry, but keep you safe. Thinking positively will open a world of endless possibilities and opportunities, but you must take certain risks to make it so.

You have a choice to make the decision that is best for you. Your thoughts are now yours. It is hard to think, let alone choose your thoughts. But you can do it, slowly. Bit by bit, every day. I believe in you.

Help Won't Come. You've to Find It

Thinking back on my life, there are things that I wanted to have. We all do. But I only wanted to have one thing in my life. I wanted to see my mom and dad at the dinner table every night. I wanted to see them when I got back from school. And most of all, I wanted to see them there for me. I wanted their support, because it was hard doing it all alone.

I know it wasn't their fault. They needed to earn a living so that I could live a better life. That is what all parents' want for their child. They want them to have a better life than them. Whatever my parents' did, they did out of love for me and my siblings.

I understand their pain, they do things that they needed to do, just so I could have a better life. But I hope that they will understand my pain.

Whether it was sports day or some competition that I took part in, I could see all the other kid's parents in the crowd. I would search for my own parent's in the crowd too, even though I knew that they couldn't come. They were always too busy with work.

So when I reach secondary school, I kind of cut back on curriculum activities. I just didn't want to be searching the crowds for them anymore. I wanted them to be there for me so much, but they just couldn't.

Every day when I came back from school, I would find the house empty. Except for my maid, nobody was around the house. I could hear only the wind, and the air-cond. It was nice and quiet to do my homework, but eventually it got depressing.

I would wondered how it would be to see them at home when I came back. Being around the house became too depressing for me to bear, so I would leave as soon as I got back from school. I would join my friends for basketball, or just hang around in the cybercafé.

Don't get me wrong, I'm not being ungrateful. My house is a lovely place to live in. But that is just what it will be, a house. My friends were my home. My house wasn't. How could it be? There was always only me.

So all I ever wanted was for some comfort, someone to be there for me. They don't need to do or say anything. If they can just be there for me during my good times and my bad, that would be enough for me.

I wasn't much of a people's person at first. My friends eventually boycotted me because I was just too rude and insensitive. Although I had no idea I was. I didn't know how they felt. I only knew how I felt. I couldn't see them from their point of view, that's how I almost lost them.

In the end, I started trying to see my behavior from their perspective. It was hard at first. But eventually I got used to it. I just imagine my feelings if someone did the same to me. Changing my point of view was all it took for me to save my friendship with them.

After that experience, I cherished them even more. I learned that help will not be given to you on a silver platter. You must find it, and get it. If you want your life to change, just change the way you look at things.

1 Mark

This is all it takes to change your grade, any grade. 1 mark can be a big difference between everything. So let me ask you, can you get 1 mark in your exams? Have you ever taken a test and failed to get one mark? I don't believe that's possible. You can't get a zero unless you didn't wrote anything on the paper.

An A is 80 marks correct? So to get an A, all you have to do is learn to get 1 mark 80 times. Getting an A is not actually hard, if you look at it this way. Getting one mark is probably easy and most of you had done it. So now, let's put a little challenge into it. If you can get 1 mark in any subject that you take, can you get another 1?

This way of thinking is much more motivational and also much more productive. It is a good way to start. You see, if it is something too easy, you won't do it. But if it is something too hard, you still won't do it. We are all alike, that's just how we are. We want to do something that we can do. But we also want a challenge. It helps us grow.

Getting 1 mark is too easy, so you won't do it. You can increase the marks you want to get depending on your target. There is no fixed amount that you need to have. You are free to choose. But make sure you feel challenged. Improvement is in our blood. We want to improve and get better. You already know how to, now show everyone that you can.

Before an exam, I would examine my previous exam paper and try to figure out which marks did I get and which ones that I didn't get. I want to know how I got them, and why I didn't get them. It is so much easier finding something if you know what you're looking for. So in this case, I was looking for more marks that I could get by using the least amount of effort possible.

I am lazy, so I'll find the simplest way to do something, and I had. So here is lesson number one. If you can change your perspective of the events in your life, you can change your way of thinking so that it may help you get the results you want. It is not positive thinking, it is selective thinking.

When you believe that you can do something that challenges you to be better than you were before, you will do it. Because this will help you grow into a much better person. Change your beliefs by changing your perspective. It won't be easy, but it is simple. It won't happen overnight, you need practice.

Control your thoughts by thinking, "How can I get another mark?" Instead of, "How can I keep my marks?" Do you see the difference in these two ways of thinking? One opens up possibilities and opportunities. If you can keep getting marks, you don't need to be afraid of losing them, because you can always get more.

If you think only to maintain or keep your marks, you will be stressed, unhappy and also feel helpless. You will feel that there is little that you can do to get those marks and you'll feel like you don't deserve them when you do. You'll feel that all you can do is prevent yourself from losing marks, not gaining them.

Your thoughts will bring you more fear. You will be scared to lose your marks. And if you don't believe you can get good results, you will believe that you can't get good results. When you don't believe, you won't even try. One mark is all it takes to start. Getting good results will be an enjoyable process only when you believe that you can get the marks, not keep them.

1 mark can be the difference between 1st and 2nd. Think about it.

Small Things Make A Difference

You now know that if you want to start, you need to believe it first. To change a belief, you just need to change your point of view. Changing just one belief can give birth to your dreams. It is often the small changes in our lives that will help us realize our dreams.

Practicing selective thinking isn't easy. It will take time for you to be aware of your own thoughts. And even more time to control what you want to think and believe. But the results will serve you throughout your life.

One raindrop can't cause a flood. But constant raindrops for long hours will. There is power even the simplest things. And so, there is power in you. You can determine more than just your results. You can choose your own life, but you have to see it first.

Never think that you are not worth it. It is a lie to think that you don't deserve to live your dreams. The small things in life always bring about the biggest impact in the long run. It is all on how you want to make that impact. So change your point of view and believe!

"If you think you're too small to have an impact,
try going to bed with a mosquito."

-Anita Roddick

CHAPTER 2:

Give Me One Reason

After I got such poor results in my first exam, of course I wanted to get better results. I did tried to study, but every time I would just put it off or go out with friends. A month was away from the mid-term exam and I didn't even studied. I didn't even know what to study, but I still wanted to get good results.

Desperately, I started asking myself, "How can I get good grades?"

Somehow, I just kept asking myself, "Why do you want to get good results?" I could think of a lot of answers for that, but none of them are actually mine. It was usually what other people told me to do.

There were plenty of reasons for other people to want me to do it, but there was no reason for me to do it. Everyone wants good result. But I just couldn't get myself to do it, because I didn't know the reason.

Then I remembered my last Moral exam. I had forgotten about my challenge that I made with myself. I wanted to get good results, but only with my own way. I didn't want to study all day and night. I didn't want to do tons of homework every day. I wanted to enjoy my secondary life while still being able to get good results.

My reason will only work for me. You may use the same reason, but there will be no guarantees that this reason will motivate you to get good results. That's why it is important for you to find your own reason.

I saw it as a challenge, as a way to do something I had never done before. I wanted to show myself that I can do things that seemed impossible to me in the past. So that's why this reason worked so well for me. It was a matter of pride, and also the excitement of a challenge.

A good reason will the spark that will light up your flame. It will be the motivation you need to persist until you succeed. So take the time to think about the reason you're using now. If you still aren't motivated by it, then it would be wise to find another reason.

Your Brain 101

Before I show you how to find your reason, let me explain something about you. Your brain is emotional, it is not logical. I can prove this too. If studying is so important and good for you, why don't you want to get good results? Most of you might answer, "I don't want to study so hard." There is more to this answer than you know.

When you think like that, it just means that you want the best for yourself without hurting yourself. How can studying hurt you? For some, it takes away their time with friends or to do something they want to do. For others, it just makes their life more complicated that it has to be. Humans are emotional creatures, because it has been our emotions that helped us to survive, not logic.

I want you to realize that when you give yourself a logical reason to study, you won't. That is just how it works, because logic can never overcome emotions. When a child is in danger, their parents will try to save him without any hesitation. If the parent had thought logically, he won't save him. To risk one's life for another, that is love. And love is an emotion, not logic.

So now you know that if you want a reason to study, it has to be an emotional one. Like me, it was about pride and the excitement of a challenge. I'll feel good when I know that I can do things that I would never thought I would do before. I saw it as an opportunity to grow and made me better than I was before.

It helps me prove to myself that I am more than what other people think I am. Most people thought I didn't know how to get good results. Others thought that I cheated for my results. I also wanted to prove these people wrong. That's why I worked for those results.

So you now know that your reason has to be an emotional reason for yourself. Your emotions will remind you and also drive you to reach your goals. That's why you need to find a good reason. It will be fun. It will be like a journey of self discovery. At the end of it, you'll learn a lot more about yourself than you know now.

A Journey Inwards

This might get a little bit personal, but I assure you that it will be for your best interest. I want you to know who you are. If not, you can't find a good reason for you to study. I'm going to ask you a series of questions, and do your best to answer it before reading on.

"If you know the enemy, and know yourself;
You need not fear the results of a hundred battles"

-Sun Tzu

What do you want to do?

Obviously, you want to get good results. But there is more to this question. I asked you what you want to do. Not need or have to do. Words can often play tricks, but more often help you discover the real you.

What do you want to do to get good results? What are the things you are willing to do to get them? Are you willing to try my methods that ensure you happiness and also good results? Are you more willing to try the safe conventional methods like studying to get good results? Both have their rewards and consequences, choose wisely.

If you want to learn to get good results, you need to let go of any negative characters. Ignorance and arrogance is not going to help you learn. You need to admit your mistakes, and know that there are much more things for you to know about. But in the end, the results will be just a satisfying as the journey you took to get them.

You can choose to study hard for your results. This way is much more simpler than learning. All you have to do is memorize everything. You don't need to know the concepts, you don't need to know the principles. All you have to know is the correct answers to the questions. For some this might be easy. But you have the freedom to choose.

My methods are nothing more than just another road for you to get travel on. It is not a shortcut. There are no shortcuts. It is another path that you can choose to take, an option. Just like the old conventional method. This path is the one less traveled by, and that is what makes all the difference.

So take your time to think about it. It may not come to you at that moment, so be patient. Keep asking yourself that question whenever you feel bored in class, before you go to sleep, when you wake up, or anytime that you have a moment to spare. Think about it.

Why do you want to do it?

If you are planning to stay up late all night to study, or try something new to get good results without the promise of it, at least have a good reason to do so. The reason that you use to do anything, shall determine your success.

Make your reasons personal. You'll be more likely to achieve your goal when you have something you care about at stake. Finding a reason is not hard actually. I usually comes down to a two categories. You'll either want to feel better, or you want to avoid feeling bad.

But there is no harm in having both. The more your reasons, the better motivated you'll be to achieve your dream. Finding a reason is simple, getting the right one is the hard part. Only you'll know if the reason is good enough for you. You'll know it because if it is the right reason, you'll wake up early in the morning to do it. You'll be doing things that you won't usually do. Most of all, you'll be satisfied doing it.

You can also use a selfless reason. You could be doing it for someone else. Or some other purpose that you would think is worth doing. There are many options for you to choose from. Explore it and find your best fit. Everyone has a different reason, you can't use other people's reason as your own. If it isn't personal, you won't be motivated to do it.

How can you do it?

This book will show you the way. In later chapters, you'll have an idea on how you are going to find your own way to get those results. But in general, you have got to have a plan.

Failing to plan, is planning to fail. Your plan doesn't have to be very detailed. It can be very simple. But nonetheless, you have got to have one. It is like a map that will lead you to your destination. Whenever you think, "How can I do it?" Just refer to your plan.

Don't be afraid to be flexible with your plan too. Things are constantly changing, so you just need to embrace that change and adapt. Be flexible. Use your imagination in solving problems along the way.

It would also be good if you write down your plan. That way, you can refer to it anytime you want. It also helps in memorizing it.

Have You Found Your Reason?

I will not sugar-coat anything here. There will be challenges when you are trying to get something you never had. That's why it is so important to have a reason to do the things that you want to do.

It doesn't matter if it is studying or getting what you want in life, a good reason is the thing that will keep you moving forward when at times seems all hope is lost. I studied the hardest during my Trial SPM, but it just didn't felt right. It wasn't something I wanted to do anymore. It was just something that I had to.

So in the end I was able to maintain my results, but there was something empty about that feeling. It wasn't the same as when I took my mid-year exam. It just didn't feel like me. I was supposed to get good results because I wanted to show myself that I can be something more than just me.

While studying for the trial, I wasn't as happy as when I learned in my Mid-Year. I was frustrated and definitely stressed. I stayed up for nights hoping to keep my results. After thinking back, that was when I realized that it was my problem all along.

I had forgotten my initial reason to get good results. I had lost my way. All I did was just to try and save my own face. It was a selfish reason, and selfish reasons often have consequences. Whatever your reason, please use this time to think of one that will work for you. And always keep your reason in your mind.

Don't worry if you are scared that it might not be the one. You already do, you just have to learn to listen to your heart. If you want to get good results using this method, you must shut out what everyone else is saying and listen to yourself.

Take a minute each day to think about your reason for getting good results. You'll know you found the right reason when you would do things that you would never do for no particular reason. Look into yourself. Go to somewhere quiet and try to rediscover yourself. It is sometimes good to be alone. That's when you find out who you really are. You can decide your own fate, just by deciding your reason.

"It is in your moment of decision that your destiny is shaped"
-Tony Robbins

The Wolf and The Rabbit

There are two type of people when it comes to attaining a goal, the wolf and the rabbit.

The wolf is the one who chases after the goal. He is hungry for it. He will do anything to have it. And also will not stop until he has it. He is driven by the goal to move towards it. He wants to succeed, and he will.

The rabbit is the passive side of the wolf. He is not driven to get something. He is driven to not lose something. Fear is his reason to move on. And so he is constantly aware of his predators. Most of the time he will be stressed and edgy. He is very careful and does his best to survive, not to thrive.

Both have different motivation to succeed. Which one do you want to be?

We have a choice, to be either the rabbit or the wolf. But we must find a certain motivation to become them.

Personally, I chose to be a wolf. I wouldn't think of not achieving my goal. I will only think to achieve it. I would do anything I could to do it. And most of all, I wouldn't give up.

But sometimes, I'll choose to be the rabbit. Fear can also be used as motivation for important matters. It will get you up and early in the morning. It will help you endure obstacles that you might face.

This is not school. So there are no right answers. You can choose either one. You can choose both. Or you can choose none at all. The choice is completely yours.

Do What You Want

When I do something because I have to, I won't be happy doing it. In fact, I might not even do it. I don't know about you, but it is certainly true for me. Is it true for you?

There have been countless times that my family told me that I should study. But I just couldn't get myself to study. The reason is simple. Because I don't like to studying. It was boring and frustrating. So I didn't studied.

Everyone tells you to get good results because you have to, but you still won't do it. That's because you might not want to do something you hate to do. I want you to get good results because you want to. That's my secret to be happy while getting good results. Because why can't you do something and be happy doing it?

When we want to do something, we tend to be more creative and efficient. Had you ever experienced doing something with so much focus, that you closed out the outside world? You would only think about what you were doing at that moment, nothing else matters. I felt that way when I'm learning and also other things as well.

I used to play basketball. And I loved that sport. But I wasn't good at it at first. I wanted to play even thought I wasn't any good. That was reason enough to get me out of bed every morning to the court. And that was reason enough to make me stay there until 7.00pm in the evening.

Even with all that time, I believe I still can improve. But one thing is for sure. I loved the sport because I love the feeling when you do good at it. Sometimes, I would be so immersed into the game that I forget the time, the people, the scores. I would just be thinking about getting the ball in the hoop.

There are occasions that I play really well. Other times I don't play that well. But the feeling I get when I play well is truly worthwhile. It is like you just know what to do at the right time. But you'll feel like you weren't the one controlling your own movements, because everything came naturally. It is a good feeling.

If you find the right reason to do something, you'll end up doing it perfectly. Being 'in the zone' is the most exciting state of mind that I had ever learnt to enter. The feeling was just amazing. I knew what I was doing. And everything just came in mind, everything went according to plan and came completely naturally. I used this state when I was taking my exams and it just went perfectly. Exams can even be kind of fun.

Passion

This is something that you can't have without. If the reason for you to do something great is passion, you just need to persist until you achieve it. Everything else will come naturally. Providence moves with you.

If you don't like to do something, you won't do it. I can put a gun in your face and make you do it, or I could let you see what you can get if you do it. Which one would you prefer?

Passion is driven by the wanting to be something more, to grow, and to contribute for others. If you have found your passion your goals, it will be easier to get them.

You must know that success is different for everyone. But to me, if you have already found your passion to achieve your goal, you had already succeeded. And I congratulate you for your success.

I Must Do It

An army sailed to a foreign land to do battle. If they had lost the war, the enemy will take over their own country, and that would be the end of their empire, their families and their home. The soldier were nervous, and the general was desperate.

When they reached shore, the general commanded, "Leave nothing on aboard!"

In a matter of minutes, the army took every supply there was on the ship. Everyone knew what was to come next.

The general burned down everyone of the ships that they had used to sail to this foreign land. "The only way back home, is to win this war! The enemy is willing to die for their country! Let's grant them their wish!" exclaimed the general.

The soldier thought about seeing their families and loved ones again. Everyone wanted to go home. But now, that 'want' became a 'must'. Each of them fought like ten men. Overpowering the enemy in will and spirit. They had won the war before it begun.

I had only took tuition for Accounts, English, Bahasa Melayu, Modern Math, Add Math, and Chemistry. I didn't go for Biology and Physic. Since I didn't have tuition for those two subjects, I had to learn them on my own. I wanted to learn Biology and Physic, but now I must because I had no help besides school. That made me learned faster.

I'm only suggesting that you don't take tuition for some of your subjects. Because too much tuition could take away your most valuable asset which is your time, unless you are certain that you learnt something there and you really need it. You don't need to agree with me completely, you have your own ways in doing things and I respect that.

I'm simply trying to tell you that you will unlock talents that you won't even know when you cut of an exit behind you. If I went to tuition, I might not have learnt the subjects. It is a sort of healthy pressure you can give yourself if you find the need to.

Sooner or later, you must turn your 'want' into 'must'. When you can do that, then you're almost there. The good results will be waiting for you.

The Man Who Had Nothing

He woke up under the bridge just before dawn. He could see the sunrise. A sign of hope for him. A sign that he could change his fate.

He looked around, and found nothing but scraps and trash. He slept among them for so long, that he became used to the sight. He wanted change, but he just didn't know how. He had nothing to his name. Not even a degree.

Walking along the streets, he saw other people busy with their lives. He saw cars that he don't even know the names to. All that he had, was a burning desire to have what he didn't have. He wanted to change his life.

Looking up to the tallest skyscraper in the city, he imagined to be up on top. Being able to look far beyond and far below. He imagined the feeling it would be when he was at the highest floor. It was fulfilling for him.

He didn't have a cent to his name, nor a lot of knowledge. But he knew two things and he told himself, "I'm dead broke. But someday, I'm not going to be!"

In him from the spark of a want, a desire had kindle the flame of a need. He need to change his life, he must. He didn't want to live like that anymore. So that was his first step. With this 'must', he started to take action. And the rest, was history.

> *"It is during our darkest moments that*
> *we must focus to see the light"*
>
> *-Aristotle Onanssis*

CHAPTER 3:

Control Yourself

"Get off the computer!! Your exam is just around the corner!" she shouted. My mom would always remind me of my exams. But at times it does seem to be unnecessary.

"The exams are a month away. I still have time to study," I replied. I had been aware of my exam date since the Trial. This was the last leg of the race.

"Whatever you say so. Just get better results," she said. I was the one taking the exam. Yet she was even nervous than me.

I did try to control myself to prepare for the SPM. But I wanted to stay on the computer more. I felt lazy wanting to prepare. I just wanted to procrastinate a while longer. But I felt good playing my games online.

Just one month away from the actual exam, I was on a stand still. The final sprint toward the end, and I was just fixed in front of my computer. The reason was simple. Because of my bad experience with my trial, I felt that preparing for the exam at a later time would hurt me less.

During my trial, I had a bad experience studying. And the results to show for it was not worth the effort. So I was scared of making the same mistakes again. I was frustrated at studying for late hours and having no improvements.

I felt good staying online and I wanted to keep distracting myself with the internet, because I didn't want to go through that pain again. So I chose not to do anything instead.

I asked myself, "Is this what I want?" My actions were not mine. It was my emotions. I knew what I wanted. And I have to discipline myself to get it. I was aware of my feelings at that time. All that was left, is to listen to them so that I can control myself once again.

"No man is free who is not master of himself"

-Epictetus

Emotions Are Guides

During puberty, it is difficult to control yourself, but you must at least try. The first step in self discipline is to know that you have control.

Your emotions are there to tell you something is wrong. Be aware of them, listen to them and find out what is wrong. Don't succumb to your emotions. Anger, fear and joy are basic emotions that you have felt throughout the years.

But now it is time to actually listen to them and make them work for you, instead of against you.

Anger is A Terrible Master

We all had wished that we had not done or said something in the past. We all have regrets that relates to anger. We feel angry when we are criticized, condemned or insulted. Then we would feel the need to do the same to others to justify ourselves. The circle continues until someone stops criticizing, but that seldom happens.

We all had lost control of ourselves once and the people we loved had to suffer for it. This is why it is important for you not to let your angry control you. It is okay to be angry. You're human. But it is not okay for your anger to let you become someone you're not.

Instead, you can control your anger. Let it serve you. Not the other way around.

Anger is A Powerful Servant

Anger has been the only thing that has ever sparked a change. Every war, every revolution in history has been caused by being too angry. They were blinded by the anger, and that led to more fighting and more deaths.

When we are angry, blood runs into the palms of our hand. It makes them hotter, allowing us to wield a weapon more easily. Our grip increases and so does the power of our muscles. Anger increases our strength. But too much, and it will you.

Less intense forms of anger are called dissatisfaction or discomfort. These are the sparks of change. This is the amount of anger you might want to have. It is healthy, as it will avoid any unnecessary violence and also might solve the problem faster.

Controlling anger might be the hardest thing to do. Because when we are angry, we tend to justify our actions and behavior. In short, we think we are right even when we are wrong. And we have our pride in the way, so it won't be easy to put down the anger.

Thinking about anger will only lead to more anger. The more your focus on something, the more it will appear. You can deal with this emotion is by distraction. If that doesn't work go to somewhere you can be alone and start counting to 100, 50 or just 10.

You can find out the reason for your anger. Not just the actions or words of another person can make you angry, the context of the words are just as important. If someone offended you, after you have cooled down. Think about the reason for the offense. You can also say that it is not what he said, but what he made you felt.

Some people offend or insults other to make themselves feel better. That's because they seldom have the privilege of being told they are better than what they think they are. Most people in today's society are like this because society has a way of putting other people down. So they just follow the crowd.

There are 2 ways to build the tallest skyscraper. You can build the tallest skyscraper, or you tear the other skyscrapers down. Putting or looking down upon others does not make your life more fulfilling. Actually it doesn't make you happy too. It just makes you feel good.

Now I want you to choose. Do you want to be someone who puts others down or someone that brings others up? You can be so much more if you only realize the choices that you have. The cause of anger, is pain.

You can even use the anger as your motivation for getting good results. Maybe someone had looked down on you. Well, prove them wrong! Don't fight them, let them eat their own words. It's okay to let someone put you down, but never put yourself down. The sweetest revenge is your success.

"Anybody can become angry — that is easy, but to be angry with the right person and to the right degree and at the right time and for the right purpose, and in the right way — that is not within everybody's power and is not easy"

-Aristotle

Nothing to Fear, but Fear Itself

On my SPM, I was scared. I was scared that I wasn't able to meet my expectations. I was scared that I would disappoint others that supported me. When I wrote my Bahasa Melayu essay, I had a mental block. I froze on the exam even thought I had written many time before.

I said to myself, "Don't be scared. You have done this before. Just think about how you did it before. Calm down. Calm down." I thought back to the steps my teacher had taught me before and the block just went away.

Being scared is normal. It kept us safe for millions of years. Anger is the fight in us. Fear is the flight in us. Being scared makes you prepare for the worst.

Being too scared, takes away that preparation. Before the exam, I had done all I can with all that I know. And I knew that if I should fail, at least I would could say, "I've done my best."

I was afraid of a lot of things in the past. I think you can relate to being afraid of heights. Being afraid is only an illusion. Let me explain.

If you say you're afraid of heights, you are actually afraid of falling down. If you say you're afraid of the dark, you're afraid of what is in it.

If you knew that you wouldn't hurt when you fall, would you still be afraid? If you knew that there was nothing in a dark room but yourself, would you be afraid?

You must have faith and believe, if you are to let go of your own fear. I learnt this when I was riding a ride in Berjaya Times Square. I believed that the ride wouldn't let me fall and had faith in the ride. So I was able to enjoy the thrill of the ride. It wouldn't be much fun if I closed my eyes after I paid for the ride, would it?

Being afraid in life can cost you a lot more than a theme park ticket. It can cost you opportunities that might never come back. Believe, do your homework and just do it. Don't think too much. Only think when you're planning or preparing. Other than that, just do it!

> *"I learned that courage was not the absence of fear, but the triumph over it. The brave man is not he who does not feel afraid, but he who conquers that fear."*
> —*Nelson Mandela*

Pain of The Past

As I have talked about in the earlier chapter, I didn't get the girl even though I transferred to the same school. I was devastated. But that doesn't mean the end of the world. Life is a continuous road of ups and downs. All you have to do is just carry on.

It won't be easy. Nothing is, but let me show you how I did it. To be fair, it was just thinking about the happy moments in my life. Without the sad moments, you won't be able to cherish the good ones.

It might sound stupid but my favorite pass time when I was a kid, was looking up into the sky while it was raining under a street light. The light would shine on the rain drops and it seemed as they were stars falling onto earth from the night sky.

Remembering that moment in my life made me realized how insignificant my problems were. Bad things will happen, it is inevitable. But you can sit there and cry about it, or be thankful for each happy moment to make up for each sad moment in your life.

Forgiving yourself is as important as forgiving others. If you say you forgive them for hurting you, but all you think about is finding a way to hurt them, that is not forgiveness. That is called revenge.

Let it go. Time will heal. Enjoy the happy moments and endure the sad ones. Be thankful that they passed. And learn from them, so that they will not happen again. Sadness is the regret we feel when we failed to do something at that moment. Your life will be full of regrets. The least you can do is make them worth it!

So whenever you can, whether it is a relationship or getting good results, give it your all. And if it ends, you could still smile with tears in your eyes and say, "I've done my best. And it was a wonderful memory." Just like anything in life, they will become memories. All you can do now is create new memories and move on.

There is not much to say on sadness. Except it will be a wonderful practice for the first skill I wanted you to learn. Think about your sad moments and find the happy moments in them. It will be there. It is always hidden. Cherish them. Don't let your past ruin your future. You still have a long way to go.

Feeling Good Isn't Being Happy

I smoked and drank before. You might ask why, and I can give you a simple answer. I didn't know the difference between feeling good and being happy, so I thought that doing those things will make me happy or at least not make me feel bad.

At first it was out of curiosity, then I started to feel better when I did it. I thought happiness and feeling good were one in the same. But I was wrong. Feeling good is immediate and temporary. Happiness takes time, but is eternal. That's why people drink and smoke. They want to feel good now.

For now, I just want you to know the difference between these two things. Happiness can be a memory, something that you can think about ten years from now and it will still be able to put a smile on your face. Like your first day in school or a funny moment in your life. I'm sure you can think of one.

It can also be appreciating the simple things in life. Like the scene of a beautiful garden, or the beauty of your loved ones. It does not require an external force or substance. Happiness comes from within.

Feeling good is instant gratification. You want to feel good now. This is why most people resort to crime. They see a shortcut, but actually it is an illusion that leads them nowhere. Other's do drugs, take alcohol or smoke cigarettes. That's why it is important that you know the difference.

Instant gratification is probably the number one problem for most students to not get good results. Think about it. You study while at home and you don't see the results you want in the exam. Even worse, you can't do the exercise your teacher give you. So you feel even worse. Naturally you want to feel good because you feel worse. So you do the things you like to do to feel that way.

So the next time you just give up studying, you'll cheat in your exams, or you'll just copy your friend's homework. You want things the easy way, but the easy way always has a price attached to it. Just like how an airplane ticket cost much more than a bus ticket. Sooner or later you need to pay what you owe.

I'm telling you this because I don't want you to end up like me. Instant gratification isn't just alcohol and cigarettes. Procrastination is also a form of instant gratification. When you put of doing some work, it just means that you want some time for yourself to feel good. Just like I had said earlier. Self-discipline is the key to control your actions. Mind over matter.

Make Your Body Feel Good

Although I don't smoke now, I'm grateful that I did. If I didn't, then I wouldn't be able to see the similarities between smoking and proper breathing.

You see, most smokers inhales the smoke and then holds it in their lungs before they exhale again. This cause more chemicals in the cigarette to go into their blood and up to their brain. So they feel light headed and much more relaxed. The chemicals had substituted oxygen in the blood.

It is the same in the proper breathing techniques used in Tai Chi, Qi Gong, and even yoga. They inhale, then hold, and then exhale. The most common count ratio is 1:4:2. They inhale for 1 second, hold for 4, then exhale for 2 seconds. You can add the ratio to 2:8:4 once you get used to it.

This breathing technique is actually very good, just don't add the cigarettes. By holding, you allow more oxygen diffuses into your blood, so your brain has more oxygen to function. You'll feel alive and more alert. Doing this 5 minutes a day can seriously change your day. I used to do this a school when I'm sleepy. It is relaxing and I makes me feel more energetic.

If you breathe properly, your body can function more properly and you can do things more productively. You'll know you breathed properly when your stomach expands while you inhale. It is also an alternative to smoking cigarettes. But don't take my words for it. Try it now! You have 5 minutes. Just count the numbers in your mind. Then feel the difference.

Besides breathing, the food that you eat is equally important. You are what you eat. But then again, you're also how you eat. So if you want your body to function better, here are a few tips. Use the one that you think is best for you.

Eat protein and carbohydrates in separate meals. Digestion is one of the most energy consuming activities that your body does every day. That's why after we eat, we don't feel like moving around much. Our body used most of its energy to digest the food we ate.

So let's use meat and rice as examples. Our saliva is a weak alkali, so our enzymes in it can digest the rice. But it doesn't completely digest all of it. The meat is not digested at all. The food is now in a weak alkali condition.

So when it goes into the stomach, it meets with an strong acid. For hours the food stays in the stomach and the protein is almost completely digested. The food is now very acidic. It then travels down to the small intestine to further digest all the remaining food and also absorb them into the body.

Our body only has a weak alkali and a strong acid. So would it take more alkali to neutralize the acid and also even more alkali to create a suitable condition to digest carbohydrates?

That's why you should not eat both carbohydrates and protein in a single meal. Eat fruits or vegetables instead, because our body doesn't digest any of those food. It only reabsorbs their nutrients and expels them. You don't have to do this every meal, just one meal a day will do just fine.

Sleep straight for long hours, not part by part. I bet that when you want to play, you would play for hours right? It is the same with your sleep. If you played for hours, or worked for hours, then sleep for hours. Not 1 or 2 hours in the class, 2 or 3 in the afternoon and 4 or 5 at night.

Make sure that you sleep in a comfortable environment, meaning make sure it is quiet and peaceful. Remember to change your bed sheets monthly and also sleep in a position that you won't regret when you wake up.

If your body hurt when you wake up, just simply change your sleeping position. Quality over quantity. 6-8 hours of proper sleep is much better than 8-12 hours of improper sleep.

Keep Smiling

Happiness is different for everyone. So I might not know what makes you happy. But we both do understand the meaning of happiness.

Trying to express happiness is like trying to tell you what plain water taste like. It is not something special. But it is part of a necessity. Let me see if I can express it well enough.

Happiness to me, is doing what you need to do while you enjoy the process as well. That is why I did what I did. Getting good results was something I needed to do. But that doesn't mean that I should not enjoy my secondary school years.

It was full of smiles and laughter. I will never forget them. It had taught me something I need to know. The 2 years had taught me to smile more often. Because we don't smile because we are happy. We are happy because we smiled. So keep smiling.

> *"Happiness is not something already made.*
> *It comes from your own actions"*
>
> *-Dalai Lama*

Listen to yourself

If you have learned anything from this chapter, learn this: listen to yourself. Only you know what is best for you, because no one on this earth is more you than you. Be willing to go against the crowd to get something that you want. In life or in school, break the status quo. Be yourself!

Of course there will be risk, but don't be afraid of them. Instead, manage them. If you're scared that's because you know there are things in which you can't control or don't know. Be prepared. Control those that you can control, and let go of those which are out of your abilities. When you do all that you can do, to the best of your abilities, everything will turn out alright. Just keep going.

So many people out there know what others want them to do but don't know what they want themselves to do. So take a moment to reflect on yourself. Think about what you want. If you want good results, then go get them. Always know that you have a choice. It is your life.

Nobody can tell you what to do, although you should listen to most of them for advice. You have a brain that can make decisions, just make sure those decisions aren't impulsive or emotional.

Usually those that are driven by emotion are selfish reason. That is because we want to protect ourselves. Being selfish and loving yourself are two entirely different things. But only a thin line between them. You can't be both at the same time. You just have to choose one. To make a good decision, you must take account the probability of success and the consequences of failure, remember that next time you decide to do anything.

Most of all, you have to believe in yourself and also trust yourself. Listen to your own opinion. Stand by your opinion even when nobody stand with you. This is what you have to do to be different. This is what you have to do to be great. Just listen to yourself.

Know that you can always do better than you were before. You can always do more. You are smarter than you were yesterday, and you'll be even smarter tomorrow. All you have to do is reflect upon yourself every day. Spend a little time a day to think about yourself.

Think about what you can do, what you could've done, and what you will do. It is a great way to know yourself even more. Do this every day, and you'll find your own uniqueness to shine brighter than ever before.

"If you conquer yourself, then you conquer the world."
-Paulo Coelho

CHAPTER 4:

Dare to Dream

My dream began when I first accepted that challenge. I wanted to prove to myself and everyone I know, that I could be more than just another student. My goal was not to be the best, but it was to be the best that I can be.

At first the dream was quite far and distant but as moved towards my dream. It started to materialize into reality. My goals which were once written on papers became my results. Goals are important because they will determine where you will go.

During my Mid-Year exam, I wanted to be better than what I was before. So I worked in that direction. In the end, that was what I had achieved. Better results.

But on my trial, I was only focused on not doing worse than my Mid-Year exam. And my efforts were directed into realizing that goal. I didn't do worse, nor did I had done better.

If you don't know how to ask, you'll never receive. These are 4 line from a poem which was written by Napoleon Hill.

I worked for a menial's hire,
only to learn, dismayed,

That any wage I asked of life
Life would have willingly paid.

Life will only give you exactly what you want. But once you had set your goals, you must be prepared to put in the effort towards it. What you ask, he will give you only that. So be careful for what you wish for.

Fortune Favors the Bold

There are a lot of things that we can't control in this world. I can't have absolute control over my results, or my life. But I do what I can. Here is a secret that I want you to know. If you commit yourself to do something, it will happen. Maybe not the way you want it to be, but it will happen.

The world is strange. It wants to find those who are different than the rest. Then it has a way of making them do things that other would not do, to get what others could not have. If you want something you never had, you need to do something you never done. Makes sense doesn't it?

I speak from my own experience to say that this is true. Everything will go your way if you commit yourself to a worthy purpose. It has been proven countless times. From the success of self-made billionaires to amazing medical miracles, it has happened.

I don't know what force it is called or how it came to be. But I know that it is there, to help you, me and everyone else. But only if you prove that you have the courage to chase after your dreams.

Don't fear what you might lose. It will only be taken temporarily. It will come back several folds of what you had lost. And also a great satisfaction in the end. The moment you succeed, will be worth all the things that you had to let go.

"Until one is committed, there is hesitancy, the chance to draw back, always ineffectiveness. Concerning all acts of initiative (and creation), there is one elementary truth, the ignorance of which kills countless ideas and splendid plans: that the moment one definitely commits oneself, then Providence moves too."

-W.H. Murray

As Simple As Possible

Whatever you do, you need to make it as simple as possible. Remembered how I've told you about changing your point of view from maintain your results to getting them? The rule of simplicity lies in there.

Making things simple will encourage you to do it. But it must be complimented with a goal. That is what gives it a challenge. And that is what will push you forward faster. It helps if you think like a child. Try to make things simple.

There is nothing wrong with thinking it will be simple. I failed my moral and got it to a B in my trial. All the way, the only think I thought was this, "How can I get more marks?" That's all you need to do. Thinking that it is simple will opens new windows of possibilities and opportunities to you.

In this case, think about how to get 1 mark first, then make it 5 or 10 if it is too easy for you. Keep going and sooner or later, you'll already have 80 marks and above.

Start somewhere that you know. Then figure out the way to something you don't know. Just keep trying. You will have help, believe me.

"When the solution is simple, God is answering"

-Albert Einstein

Leverage

I'm a lazy student. I always find ways to do the most with the least amount of effort. It has seemed that I am used to doing things like that. So how can you get more by doing less?

Well, for our exams there are certain topics that are very popular. They appear most of the time, so why not focus on those topics first if you were to start? Leverage and laziness both start with an "L" and I don't think that it was just coincidence.

If your results were anything like mine in the beginning of the year, then this is the best method for you to practice if you want to get started. First you've got to find the things that can make the most difference in the papers that you are taking.

It is simple. You just put 5 years of the past year SPM of any subject in front of you, and analyze through them. Just note down the similarities based on topics and this will help you get a clear study for you.

I learnt this by reading book about business. The smallest change can make a big difference in your results. Just like how you kick a football. If you kick it from a certain angle, you make it go a fixed direction. That one small difference in angle will be the difference in the direction of the ball. Think about it.

To have made that massive improvement of my results, I simply did less to get more. I listened to the tips that teacher gave out and the one's that my friends gave out. Then I analyzed the past year papers and found the similar topics. All that was left was to learn the topics and be ready for my good results.

It is that simple, but only if you want it too. If you don't, I can't stop you now can I? Whatever you do, make sure you do it because it will make you happy and help you achieve your goal.

Leveraging isn't being lazy, it is being productive. Every business wants to do more with little, if you can do that with yourself. You won't have a problem helping other people do the same.

> *"I choose a lazy person to do a hard job. Because a lazy person will find an easy way to do it."*
>
> *-Bill Gates*

80-20 Rule

This is a principle that they should teach in school. This is the Pareto principle. 20% of any effort will lead to 80% of the results.

This is usually used in business, but I don't see why it can't be applied in school. As an example, 20% of the sales make 80% of the profit. In school, especially in your exams, 20% of your effort will give you 80% of your results. The other 80% of your efforts will bring you 20% of your results.

That's why for some of you, it is hard to increase your marks. You keep on doing the 80% of work that leads to 20% of the results. Finding out how to get more from less is easy. Just ask yourself, "What can I do to increase my results without much effort?" Think about it long enough, and the most suited answer will be given to you. You are never alone.

It was this question that I had kept asking myself over and over again that lead to me discovering this principle. So look at past SPM topics and see for yourself which topic will give you the highest return if you fully study it.

Usually there would be 2 or 3, but choose the ones that you want to learn. It doesn't matter which you choose as long as you choose the one that you are interested in, everything will go according to plan.

The Difference That Makes The Difference

Have you ever tried to burn a leaf with a magnifying glass? Without the magnifying glass, the heat energy from the rays can't converge into a single point. The leaf won't burn.

The thing that separate's those that succeed and those that don't is simple this one word: "Focus". Do you think it is hard to focus? Do you think it is hard to change your focus? Then let's have a little exercise shall we?

Look around your room and try to find the things that are red. Remember the shape of the object and put that image in your mind. Remember as many as you can. This is to test your focus. Come on, try to remember as many red as you can.

Now, try remembering the objects that were black in color. Can you recall most of the objects that were black, or do you see more red colored objects in your mind? That is the power of focus. And you can change that focus easily. All you have to do is be aware.

Imagine if you focused on the unimportant things. You would only see more of them wouldn't you? Just like how you would see more red colored objects if you focused on just the red colored objects. Choose wisely what to focus.

Try focusing on the things that matter, the 20% that'll make the 80%. You should put all your focus on the sections that give the highest marks and not all of them. Work at one section at a time.

There are advantages to focusing. One of them is that you won't feel so overwhelmed. If you prioritize carefully and work hard at it, you will instantly see the results in the coming exam and feel more encouraged to do get more marks on your next exam.

Another benefit would be that you'll be able to get things done quickly while still having extra time for yourself. It helps lighten your burden. Wouldn't you want that?

You've to Walk Before You Run

You can't reach a mountain without passing the valley. The bad times that you face are just as important as the good times. They teach you something that you don't know, that's why you failed. Don't worry, it happens. It is a chance to be better, to improve, and to learn.

Never run away from your failure. You have to embrace it because your life is going to be filled with it. When you see them as lessons, then you'll learn to grow and improve yourself. That will bring you more happiness than you can imagine.

The difference between school and life is this. School teaches you the lessons and punishes you if you fail. Life punishes you when you fail and teaches you the lessons. The only thing to do is move on. Because that is what life is all about.

I believe that the purpose of you being alive right now is to give your life a purpose. It is not true for just me, but also for everyone else. My brother once asked me a question I had long ago asked myself.

He came to me on a night and asked with eyes about to burst into tears, "Why are we here for!? Why do we live if we have to die?" To tell the truth, I couldn't give him an answer. I didn't know it myself. But I know one thing, if I'm going to die anyways. Then why not make it a life worth living?

I want you to live the life you want because I think you deserve it! Who is to say you can't live that way? Don't let others put you down. They say something because they can't do it themselves. Don't be angry at them. Show them that they can do it. Inspire them.

Without a bad side, you wouldn't be able to remember the good times now would you? Live your life the way you want to. Same goes for your results. If you want to get good results, aim high! But learn to walk before you run. Take baby steps and start small.

The View is Nicer on Top

There is just something about being on top of a mountain or hill that gets me excited. I love to be at high grounds. It allows me to look down and see the path that I have traveled. It makes me feel proud of myself to know how far that I have come.

But being on top doesn't only let me see what is below me. It lets me see what is in front of me and above me. When you are on top of a mountain, you'll find that there are other mountains to climb.

And if you've been to Mt. Everest, then you might think of going beyond. You would want to go to space or dive into the deepest seas. Whatever you do, I can bet that you'll do it out of excitement and challenge.

We want to improve, that is in our DNA. But keep in mind that we can never reach our fullest potential, because we are limitless. After you get the results you want, you'll definitely want more than just that. But how can you improve more if you don't know how to, am I right?

I would rather burn as brightly as I can for a moment than to live in the darkness forever. There isn't much joy in hiding your talents and dreams. We feel best when we use our talents and make our dreams into reality. Don't let anyone tell you that you can't. You can!

Life is all about choices. Your choices will determine the life you'll live.

> *"What is the point in being alive if you don't at least try to do something remarkable?"*
>
> *-Mario Novak*

Putting It All Together

This is the final chapter for yourself. The next chapter will be totally on learning to get good results. The first 4 chapter are your foundation to achieving anything in life. You can say that it is part of the success formula. But it is not the success formula. There are many more.

There are many roads to success. The first 4 chapters had shown you some. Remember these lessons if you want to achieve anything great in your life, and all will go your way.

1. Believe That You Can

You won't do anything if you don't believe you can do it. Change your point of view so that you convince yourself to believe.

Start small, start from somewhere you are familiar with. Then work your way up.

2. Find A Good Reason

You will need to believe to get you started. But you need a good reason to keep you going. You don't just have to find one. Find more if you can, that will be even more motivation.

Think about them twice a day, when you wake up and also before you go to sleep. Motivation is required daily to keep you focused on where you want to go. Don't worry about getting there, you'll know how.

3. Emotions Are Guides

You know yourself better than anyone else knows you. So listen to yourself! If you're unhappy, angry or scared find out why. Know the exact reason to it. Don't let your emotions control you.

Practice to control them, start by being aware of them. Noted down some of the emotions that you feel throughout your day. Then you can better understand them and find out the cause for them.

It won't be easy, but don't worry. This is not a test, you won't fail. You will only keep getting better. Make some time alone to reflect on yourself. Find out who you are. Then you'll know who you want to be.

4. Think Big

Have the courage to go against the crowd. Have the strength to do what others could not do. You have more power than you realize. Don't be afraid of it. Embrace it! Getting good results will only prove that you have much more to offer.

Never blend in the crowd. Similarity is boring. Be different, be extraordinary, and most of all, just be you.

Find that 20% of effort that will give you 80% of the results. Working hard is good, but it takes too long. Know what to work hard for! Don't keep doing things that won't bring you any results. It will be just a waste of time.

CHAPTER 5:

Learn

"You seriously don't know how to wrap a book!?"

"No actually, I haven't wrapped a book before," it was kind of embarrassing for me to admit that, at least I was answering honestly. I was 16 and I didn't know how to wrap a book.

"How did all your books in the past were wrapped!?" asked Jermaine.

"My mom. My aunt. My maid." I looked down on a book, 'The Hunger Games' and got an eagerness to learn.

"Can you teach me how to wrap a book?" I asked as I swallowed my pride.

"I can't teach you without wrapping paper."

"I'll bring some tomorrow. Do we have a deal?" I smiled and offered a my hand. She shook mine as a sign of agreement.

'The Hunger Games' was the first book that I wrapped. It wasn't perfect when I learnt to wrap it the first time, but with practice I began to wrap better. Now, I love to wrap every book that I buy, that's because I know of the importance of books. It was books that inspired me to inspire you. It was books that drove me into writing this book.

Studying needs hard work. Learning needs character. All you need to start, is curiosity and humility. There is only one way to study, you memorize everything in the book. But there are many ways that you can learn. That's why learning is so much more fun and exciting.

Some students feel overwhelmed at school because most of the time, the school only uses one method for students to learn. They ask that students study. That's why some students might not catch up with the classes. They don't learn by studying. They learn differently. Each student is unique, and that's why it is important for you to know the best way for you to learn, so that you can get good results.

Studying is Not Learning

Studying is just one way of learning. Just think about it, when was the first time you learnt to use Facebook? Did you study for it?

There are so many things that you have done by learning than by studying. Was it fun to learn to use Facebook? I bet it sure was. When you know how to learn, you can do anything. Just like I have said earlier in the book, the world today belongs to those who can learn, unlearn and relearn.

Learning doesn't take long. You learn something at that very moment and you will remember it forever. Some of you might study for nights and yet still don't get what the topics in the textbooks are saying. If you have that problem, then let me show you how to learn.

You might think that this is obscured. Obviously you know how to learn, but do you know how to control it and apply it to anything or anytime you want? I mean, do you know how to learn anything at anything you want?

Learning isn't about being right. It is about being better than you were before. You aren't competing for anything. You just feel like improving yourself to enrich your own life and hopefully the lives of others around you.

However there is a price to learning. Ignorance and arrogance are not suited for learning. That is why I wrote the first part of the book. I want to help you control the impulses and prepare you for the learning process.

If you feel like you have already known everything that you can know. Then my knowledge will be of no value to you. But if you read on with an open heart and mind, you might find more than just knowledge, you might learn how to create knowledge.

"If you think education is expensive, try ignorance."
-*Derek Bok*

Knowledge is Not Power

Knowledge is only potential power. You can have all the knowledge in the world but you still wouldn't be able to achieve anything if you don't do something.

Some students feel frustrated with school because of this. They know that they only learn the knowledge but they see no application for it. They want to know how do you use this in real life, to make their lives better. But the school disappoints because they only give you knowledge, what you do with it is not their concern.

Many students are lost because they don't know what to do with the knowledge even though they had acquired it.

"When am I going to use this in the real world!?" Students wants to know how you can apply things that you learnt in school to their lives, but many school failed to show the application. They just follow the textbook.

Learn and Grow

If you have learned something, don't you feel a need to use it? Like a new football move, or a new app, you would want other people to know that you can do it. And most importantly, you want yourself to know that you can do it.

Learning is self-improvement. It feels good to know that you were better than before, it gives us a sense of accomplishment. That is why I just loved to learn. Growing up means learning new things that you had never learned before. You can learn new things and get better at doing the old things that you knew.

Without learning and growing, you would feel like you're getting nowhere, like there is just something missing. It is a hunger for growth. Besides our own body, our mind also needs to grow.

Our mind is like a muscle, use it more often can it grows. If you haven't used it, then it will remain small. Thinking and imagining are ways you can exercise your mind. Studying however, is not.

You don't want to just memorize things. You want to understand them and know them. If you can't understand them, then you feel like you had failed to learn them. Don't be discouraged. You just need to try a different approach.

How Do You See The World?

So to learn, you have to get new information before applying it. How do you get new information?

First, you have to use your eyes. You can read about something to get new information. This is what the school wants you to master. Luckily, you did. If you didn't you wouldn't be able to read this book.

Second, you can use your ears. Hearing the morning radio for news is the same as listening to your teacher in the classroom.

You need to listen to what others have to say based on their own experiences and the facts they had gathered.

Lastly, you have to do it. You have to feel it, apply it. Before the time of written text, men have learnt by this method. This is the act of applying. We learn the best with this method because it is literally in our DNA.

So, after I have shown you these 3 methods. Which ones do you think you are best at? The one you choose is the way you see the world but remember, you can always choose more than one.

You Look but You Don't See

If you're good at reading you are strong in this point. But I'm not going to teach you how to see. I'm going to show you the difference between two much forms of seeing. There are visualization and observation.

Observing is not just looking, you analyze with your brain but you look with your eyes. You receive new information by observing someone doing something. An example would be a workout in the gym.

You would let the one who knows what they are doing go first. Then you would observe the position of their body with the workout instrument. Later you just copy doing whatever workout the other guy just did.

The difference between looking and observing is so small, that I wouldn't blame you if you didn't notice it. In fact, it took me quite a while to put this in words too.

When you're observing, your mind is at work. It is taking in new information and processing it. It sends impulses to your muscles to mimic the movement of the other person. But when you are looking, your mind is not a work. Your eyes are just simply taking in the light reflected by the object.

For boys, have you felt the urge to try those Kung-Fu moves in Jackie Chan's movies when you were little? That is when your body has observed and wants to repeat the movement to show you that you've learnt it. Although you might need a lot of practice before being able to do everything Jackie does. But you get the idea.

In school, you can apply it to math. After you've seen someone found a solution to a math problem, observe. Take in the information by seeing the difference in workings and also ask for principles of the topics.

It's the fastest way to learn math. But you have to let go of your ignorance and arrogance. It may be a little too much to ask, considering it is impulsive. But the first step is to be aware of it. The more you are aware, the better your control.

Visualization is used throughout this book. I have written this book purposely in story form to the best of my abilities so that you can practice visualization. You have no problem in visualization if you made it this far in the book. Congratulations.

Now, imagine an apple. That is visualization. Imagine a pink elephant with green tusk riding on a bicycle on its way to Kuala Lumpur. That is visualization right there. It happens in your mind.

The image vividly appears in your mind with colors and movement. The clearer the image, the more focused you are at visualizing. Now, imagine you getting straight A's for your SPM. See yourself going on stage being congratulated by teachers and friends.

See your parents sitting there cheering as you get your results. Every second seems worth cherishing doesn't it? This is how I used to remember facts. I find this method very exciting and fun, most importantly it is effective.

Our mind remembers best if you make it into a movie mixed with a little emotion. The stronger the emotion links to the images, the stronger the memory. In short, you remember best when you feel something after you had seen something.

When you see a ghost movie, don't you remember the scary parts much better? That's because it is in the form of a movie and you feel scared. So why not use this method to memorize dates, places, and also people?

For example, when you want to remember a historical event, go on Google and search for images of the place. Then pick one for you to link the event on it. Let's say there is a war in the jungle. So, all you have to do it just imagine a war in the place you seen on the image you found Google.

It would be like directing your own movie in your head. Name the lead characters, supporting characters and the setting of the place. Visualizing is memorizing having fun.

For numbers, try to remember 4 at once. You remember best when you chunk the numbers into groups of four. I find this to be true for me and most people, so you can try it out. Remember dates in 4 numbers but not more, you can choose to remember less.

For new words, split them based on their syllabus. For memorizing a sentence, 4 words in a chunk. It might be hard for some to visualize to here are the examples:

72015678718927384192
7201-5678-7189-2738-4192

Conviviality
Con-vi-via-li-ty

The more you get the hang of it, the more things you'll be able to memorize. Some have natural stronger memory than others, but that doesn't mean those who don't have that gift can't be good at memorizing too. You can train it just like you can train your muscles.

Visualizing will definitely fix whatever you want to memorize into your brain as long as you think of the image. I have shared all I know about our gift of sight. Let us move on to the next sense that helped us see the world, shall we?

> *"Small is the number of people who see with*
> *their eyes and think with their minds"*
>
> *-Albert Einstein*

You Hear But You Don't Listen

I went for a camp last year and one of the activities they had us do was to walk back to camp by following a string that will to lead us back to camp. It was midnight and all of us were sitting on the side of a road in groups waiting for our turn. The instructor only gave one instruction, "Don't break the string."

The string will lead us back to camp, providing that it doesn't break. At that moment, it was dark and I was tired. I had to find my way back to camp with the help of the string. I listened and followed the instructor's advice and went back into the camp. He didn't need to say much. The instruction was clear and simple. Don't break the string.

When you don't know what to do, usually you will recall any advice that you had heard of. But hearing them doesn't mean you actually listened now do you? The difference between these two is all in the mind.

To listen, you have to focus on your target. This is call paying attention. Usually those who are good at listening are very good in music. They play instruments quite well and have excellent pitch.

You don't have to be a musician to be good at listening. Some people are great communicators. They have the talent in listening for points and making connections between the words that were spoken throughout the conversation.

They know the difference in pitch and tone and can manipulate theirs as well. They can make you feel comfortable every time they open their mouths. Even their presence might be enlightening. These people often grow up to be leaders.

If you want to have a better relationship with anyone, this simple advice will definitely get you there. Everyone loves to feel like they are being listened to. That's why it is considered rude to talk when someone else is talking. But for me, if they want people to listen, then they must listen to the other person first.

Listening is the fundamentals in human relations. Good listeners have a number of friends that will be helpful for them in school and later in life. But they must know how to differentiate each one and try to push themselves and the other person to their fullest potential.

If you have good results and you have a remarkable ability to listen, then please share your knowledge with others. When you listened to someone, they will listen to you. Just have a bit of patience.

Listening to instructions such as steps for writing an essay or even workings for math can be a great asset. But remember to jot it down if you feel like you can't remember all of them. Listen to stories and share your knowledge in story form as much as you can if you want others to know what you know.

You might not be able to do much for yourself, but you certainly will do a lot for others. You are a great asset to anyone who comes near you. Think of yourself as a search engine. Some people are shy and want to know certain information, you can assist them.

You transfer information verbally, meaning by telling them. You could be the one asking the teachers for solutions, or asking one of the smart students in school. Share your knowledge with others and your results will certainly increase in no time. Because if you can explain it simple enough, that means you've already understood it.

This is what I meant by everyone has a gift. You don't always have to refer to a book, you can get information by exchanging information. You can help others along the way using your talents. This is certainly a rare talent in today's society. If you are good at listening, keep on listening.

> *"We have two ears & one mouth so that we*
> *can listen twice as much as we speak"*
>
> *-Epictetus*

Talk is Cheap

I can sit here all day and talk about something but still I can have no idea what I'm talking about if I don't show it. If I can convince someone that I know something, then I have learned it.

Getting information is just one part of the whole learning process. If you really want to learn something and you want to make it stick, then you have to show someone that you do know it.

I advise you to show someone because often we are bias about ourselves. If you can stand the feedbacks from other people, you have no problem learning anything again in your life. Often this is the hardest part. Keep in mind that showing others that you have learned something is not the same as showing yourself.

If you have a talent in seeing, you can show them with words on a paper. If you are good at listening, you can tell them. But what if you aren't good at both of these? Then you have to show it to them. Apply what you have learned.

If I just told you that I got good results without studying, would you believe me? Or course not! I need to convince you and that has been my greatest challenge in writing the book. Showing others your way of thinking is not as easy as it sounds. But it is rewarding once they understand.

The only trick to show someone that you know what you're doing is to use it to help them. People don't remember what you did for them as much as how you made them feel. It all comes back to the heart. That's why if you have read the earlier part of the book, you might understand this more. Only help when needed.

Showing someone you have learned something is not about showing off. It is about making a confirmation to yourself that you know what you are talking about. Your actions doesn't define who you are, your motive does. Most people have a sixth sense when you try to put on a show. Be sincere in your approach and you'll do just fine.

If you say you know how to get good results in a subject, go and get it. Don't keep giving yourself excuses. That is what losers do! Don't run from your mistakes, face them head on! If you admit your mistakes, you'll learn from them and be better next time. Don't let your pride blind you.

This holds true in life as well. If you want to get anywhere in life, then you have got to admit your mistakes. Life will throw a lot of walls at you. Don't find another way around it. Tear down the wall or punch a hole through it. Fortune favors the bold. This is the reason only a few can get what they want in life.

Practice Makes Perfect

Overall, there is actually one way to be good at something. You have got to practice it. I could get every information about playing a piano, but unless I actually played a piano, I won't be good at it.

However, if you do something without know some information before hand, you might run in to unnecessary obstacles. Making it simple. You have got to know what you're doing, then you have got to do it.

If you can do this, the trial and error process will be shorter. You'll save more time and learn faster. This is what I mean by learning. You have got to know how to leverage and focus your resources to save energy and time. Isn't this better than studying?

For this to work, you've got be willing to admit to your mistakes and know that improvement has no limit. You can always better. You can always improve. So be humble and learn! It is fun and also beneficial.

Who knows? Maybe you will be the one changing the world.

"Live as you were to die tomorrow,
Learn as you will live forever."

-Mahatma Gandhi

Relearn and Unlearn

There is no shame in relearning something you had already known. I learnt this the hard way. I thought after my PMR, I would still be able to catch up in subjects. I thought it would all be the same, so I had enjoyed my Form 4 without much caring about my results.

But I was wrong. It was quite a lot to catch up on in Form 5. No matter how good that you think you are at something, you will still not know something. There is no shame in that. Just relearn.

To unlearn, you need to let go of past ideas that are no longer suited for this age. We had gone from the Industrial Age to the Information Age. The change is so fast that most people had failed to see it. If you want to keep up with the constantly changing economy, then you need to learn, unlearn and relearn, or you will get left behind.

It is okay to not know everything. It is okay to be wrong. Just shallow your pride and admit it. That is life, you make mistakes and grow. But you need to admit your mistakes first, like how I had admitted mine.

I really want to help you to get good results. But I can't do that unless you are willing to help yourself too.

Here is What I Did

Be completely aware and focused when your teacher is teaching. But I didn't do it all the time. Most of the time, I was either sleeping or somewhere else in the school. But when I do learn, I visualized a kind of movie in my mind. Especially for the science subjects.

For languages and also history, I memorize new words and points for essay using the same kind of visualization. Make the movie in your mind colorful, attractive, and also include sound in it.

For math, I always start with something that I know. Then I slowly try to link it something that I don't know. Always ask if you don't know something. Learn the principles of math, not the methods. You can do a lot more with the concept and principles.

For my moral, I guess I just read a lot of books and newspaper and memorize the things that need to be memorized. Most of the answer are either repeated or similar, so I don't think you would have much problem with that if you are aware of your paper.

For accounts, I always know who I am. I change my point of view from banker, debtor, and business man. So that I know which are my assets, liabilities, income and expenses. It is kind of fun actually.

I learn best using my sense of sight. So I take in information using my eyes. Then gather the information in my mind to be processed by myself. I then practice until I was good at a certain subject. If I didn't know something, I would ask. Sounds easy doesn't it?

Overall, you have to be aware when you learn. Find out what you don't know and what you know. Memorize only when absolutely necessary. Make movies in your mind to remember points and also concepts. Always ask. Lastly, never stop learning.

Be Willing to Make Mistakes

I have made my fair share of mistakes in my secondary life that I am sure most of you can relate to, but that was not my biggest mistake. My biggest mistake was not being able to show those that were closest to me that I cared.

If I was not inconsiderate, insensitive and arrogant, I would have been able to done more. I would have been able to show them that I appreciate them. I took a lot of things for granted one of them was my family, the other were my friends.

I am sorry to my mother and father, I could have been a better son. I know I am not the son that you have always wanted. I know that I can do better and I will. Sorry for being rebellious and thank you both for always supporting me in the things that I have done. I love you.

Kin Tung, Kee Guan, Jun Zhi, Ryan and Daven, I am sorry that I was not the best friend that you guys deserve to have. I know that I am hot tempered sometimes, but I am controlling myself. I hope that all of you can see that I am trying. Thank you for boycotting me 2 years ago. It made me reflect upon myself and also learn to be more grateful for all of you.

These 5 years of secondary school has been the best 5 years of my life. The memories will live in me forever. Grades are important, but there are things which are more important than that. Family and friends will always be there for you. You will not be needing the results after you have gone to further your studies or applied for a job, but you will need the support that your family and friends can give you. To me, that is more important than all the A's that I can ever have.

There is also someone very important to me that I want to thank. He is my mentor and teacher. Without him, I would have not been able to do what I have done today. Although he was not good in his studies, he shared his philosophies in life with me. He is 2 years older than me and he is currently working. I told him one day that I would come back to find him, that would be the day that I have truly succeed in life and that I can help him the same way he helped me. Thank you, Khai Yaw.

Admitting that you have made mistakes does not make you weak or imperfect. In fact, it is the other way around. If you admit to your mistakes and learn from them, if you change for the better because of them. Then you are really learning and growing. That is what I want to emphasize here in this book. To get what you want from life, the price is a simple one. Life simply wants you to learn and grow. So go out there and the better than you were before! You can do anything as long as you are willing to learn and grow.

Afterword

Your time in reading this book is very much appreciated. Thank you for your time. I hoped that this book has helped you in some way to get good results and also change your outlook on life.

Some books are meant to be finished, others to be digested. This book has shown you a success formula that has been proven over time to work. It gave you the potential to succeed. Now you must learn to apply this knowledge.

Your future is yours. And I hope that you will shape your own future to the way you want it to be. You are a genius. Never forget that.

A Return to Love

Some of you might think that you still can't do it. That's because the school system has taken away your imagination. When you have a wild idea, you were criticized of being illogical. With every criticism, you doubt yourself more and more.

Some of you have completely given up believing that you can be something you are not. Our society is a product of hundreds of years of unchanged schooling system. We have developed a certain way of thinking. We believe that not everyone is a genius. Everyone is labeled and you can't change who you are.

That is so not true. We are all geniuses, just not all the same. Don't let people tell you that you're not! Don't think you aren't because of your exam results! And never let yourself believe that you are not worthy of achieving anything in life.

Some have natural talent in learning the way the school teaches. Others have talents outside of school. Like music, art and sports. They are geniuses, but not in school. So it is only natural for them to do the things that they are good at and also enjoy doing. Why should we judge them for that?

Don't be scared to change. You have more power than you realize. I believe that if students can't learn the way we teach, then we should teach the way they learn. Do you agree?

"Our deepest fear is not that we are inadequate. Our deepest fear is that we are powerful beyond measure. It is our light, not our darkness, that most frightens us.
-Marianne Williamson

Which Genius Are You?

Howard Gardner, developmental psychologist and professor of cognition and education at Harvard Graduate School of Education, categorized intelligence into seven main types: Verbal-Linguistic, Logical-Mathematical, Body-Kinesthetic, Spatial, Musical, Interpersonal, and Intrapersonal.

1. Verbal-Linguistic

In short, these are those who are good at reading, writing, and also story telling. They do well in school, especially in language. They can gather information from any passage you give them. They are good in literature. They are most likely to become journalist, authors, teachers and poets. Those who are blessed with this intelligence are the star students in school.

2. Logical-Mathematical

They are good at looking at numbers and are human calculators. They understand the relationship between two premises and can make a solid conclusion based on it. They are very logic based. They do well in science and math of any kind. They usually become engineers, accountants, mathematicians and physicians. They are also recognized by the school.

3. Body-Kinesthetic

Sports are their main thing. They feel more comfortable by doing. They learn by touching, feeling and experiencing. Most athletes have this intelligence. They know their body well and can control it better than the average human. They become famous athletes, dancers and coaches. They shine best in the field of sports or bodily expression.

4. Spatial

They see the world by seeing. They remember faces, roads, images and places very well. Colors always catch their eyes. They can imagine the space it takes to build a tower. It is a visualizing ability. They can see what others cannot. Architects, designers and artist share this intelligence. They turn the 2D into 3D. They create our world.

5. Musical

Their assets are their ears. They can easily learn to play any instrument they come in contact with. They can identify pitches just by listening. They are very attentive to the way you say the words as well as the words you're saying. They become musician, members of a band or play in a symphony orchestra. They fill our world with music of us to express our emotions by songs.

6. Interpersonal

This is the trait of leaders. The ability to persuade, influence and get along with anyone who comes in contact with them. They understand how you feel, they can make you feel the way they want you too. These usually become politicians, CEOs, presidents and such. They find the best in others and can gather different people to work together to achieve a common goal.

7. Intrapersonal

This is the last and the most important of all the intelligence. You can have only this intelligence but still be able to outperform those that have the above 6 intelligence. This is the emotional intelligence. This is the key to success.

What do you say to yourself when you're scared, angry, frustrated or sad? Do you know what you're feeling and the reason behind it? How do you react when you face setbacks or when someone mistreats you? Are you good at delaying your gratifications?

Those who have high intrapersonal intelligence simply have no problem with it. They can identify and control their emotions. They can find the best way possible to achieve their goals. They find the pleasure in life and live in a world full of hope and happiness. More importantly, they make those who are close to them better persons. They never stop learning. Self-discipline is their specialty.

What we learn in school are only Verbal-Linguistic and Logical-Mathematical intelligence. The geniuses in schools have only 2 of the 7 intelligence. They are not promised success after they complete their education.

From birth, you're granted some of these intelligences. Get to know your inner genius. Remember, you can have more than one. Know how you learn and don't stop learning. Life is an ongoing lesson. Every day you are smarter than the day before you. Every day you are a step closer to your dream. Every day you are given a blessing that so many others do not get. Use your time well.

Imperfection is Our Perfection

Man's greatest weakness is his greatest strength. And our mind is the key to changing that weakness into our strength.

That is why optimism is one of the traits of the successful ones. You see, we are imperfect for a reason. That reason is simple. It is for us to learn and grow, to improve. If we are perfect, what is there left to improve?

Imagine if everyone was. There won't be any wars, and there will be peace, but at a price. No one would need our help. Everyone would have nothing to do. They would have no purpose in life. There won't be any dissatisfaction, so there won't be any improvement.

That's why I say that you hold in you a power so great that it can shake the world. Your limitless capacity for improvement is the greatest treasure you can have. You just need to harness this power by controlling your mind. And the first step to that is to learn. Once you have mastered learning, you can do anything you want. There will be no limit to the goals you can accomplish.

Isn't this a wonderful gift? Your power is only limited by your mind. And this is what I want to give to you. I want you unlock yourself from your own cage. The criticism of society has made you doubt yourself. Well, I'm here to tell you that you have that power and if you can prove it to me by getting good results using the things I taught you in the book, then you have to prove to yourself that you are a genius.

As I have said before, this book is nothing more than another road for us to travel. This road will only lead you beyond good results and to the life you want it to be only if you let it do so. It is okay to let someone else tell you that you can't do something, but don't let yourself do the same thing.

Our imperfection is our perfection. We can be whatever we want to be. So why not be someone that can help other people? The world needs you, they need a hero. Someone needs to make the world a better place. You can be that person.

You already know how. The question now is, "Would you let yourself do it?"

"To laugh often and much;
To win the respect of intelligent people
and the affection of children;
To earn the appreciation of honest critics
and endure the betrayal of false friends;
To appreciate beauty, to find the best in others;
To leave the world a bit better, whether by a healthy child,
a garden patch or a redeemed social condition;
To know even one life has breathed easier because you have lived.
This is to have succeeded."
-Ralph Waldo Emerson

My Last Gift

This is nothing much. It is just simple poem that I wrote to help me in my exams. I wish to share it with you, and I hope that it will help you in your exam just as it had helped me in mine.

I will not know what happens next,
But I know what I will do.
Tomorrow, I will do my best;
Today, I will tell the truth.

Good luck in your life.

ABOUT THE AUTHOR

Calvinn Tay Chok Hong was born on November 1996 in Kuantan, Pahang.

He was educated in SJK(C) Semambu until 2008. He furthered his education in SMK Semambu before transferring to SMK Teluk Chempedak. He then later transfer to SMK Alor Akar and took his SPM there. He is currently taking the America Degree Program at Taylors Lakeside University.

This is his favorite quote:

"I have noticed even people who claim everything is predestined,
and that we can do nothing to change it,
look before they cross the road."

-Stephen Hawking